Y0-CCV-251

Table of Contents

CHAPTER 1

Rocks in Space

Our solar system is made up of the Sun, eight planets, and many moons. The planets **orbit**, or travel around, the Sun. The moons orbit the planets.

our solar system

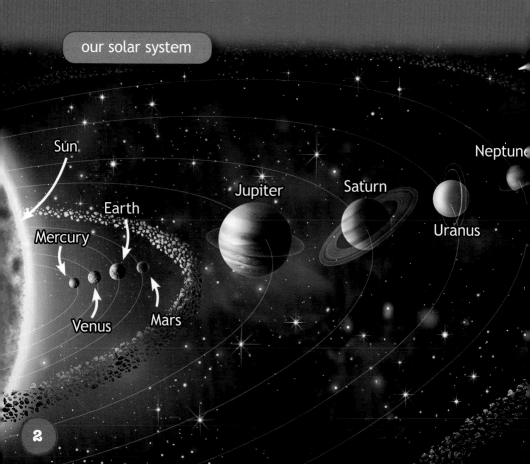

Sun

Mercury

Venus

Earth

Mars

Jupiter

Saturn

Uranus

Neptune

Some of the planets are made of rock. In fact, Earth is sometimes called the third rock from the Sun. But it is a very BIG rock!

rock planets

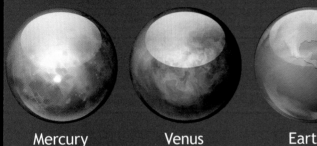

Mercury   Venus   Earth   Mars

Rock is the hard material that makes up Earth's surface.

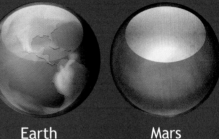

Earth's rocky surface

Our solar system is full of other rocks, too. These are called **space rocks**.

SMART WORDS

orbit: to travel around something, like the Sun or a planet

space rock: an object in space made of rock, ice, gas, dust, or metal

space rocks

3

What Is a Space Rock?

A space rock is exactly what it sounds like: a rock in space. Space rocks are pieces of rock and other materials, smaller than planets. Some can be tiny. Others are much bigger.

space rocks

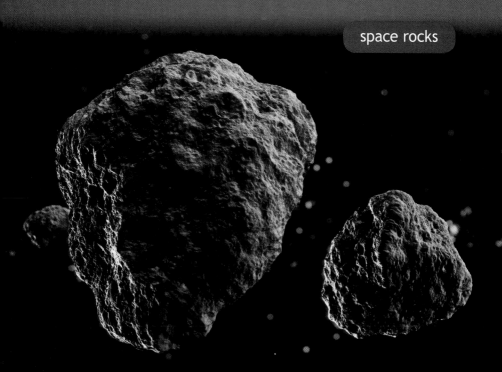

Space rocks usually stay in space. But sometimes they enter Earth's atmosphere. That's the layer of air that surrounds our planet.

atmosphere

Earth's atmosphere

When they do, they usually catch fire and burn up. But sometimes, little chunks of rock make it all the way to the ground.

SMART WORD

atmosphere: the layer of air that surrounds a planet

SMART WORDS

Fill in each blank with a Smart Word.

> atmosphere   space rocks   orbit

Most _____ burn up before they reach Earth.

The layer of air that surrounds a planet is called its _____.

atmosphere

Earth

Earth's atmosphere

Planets _____ the Sun.

TALK LIKE A SCIENTIST

Explain to a friend why most space rocks do not crash into Earth. Use your Smart Words **atmosphere** and **space rocks**.

SPACE ROCKS DISPLAY

You will need:
- paint
- paintbrush
- stones and rocks
- shoe box
- star stickers

1. Collect stones and rocks of different shapes and sizes.

2. Paint them different colors such as brown, black, and gray to look like space rocks.

3. Paint the outside and inside of the shoe box black.

4. Decorate the shoe box with the star stickers.

5. Put your space rocks inside the shoe box.

6. Label the box Space Rocks.

7. Display your space rocks.

CHAPTER 2

Odd Balls in Space

Asteroids are kinds of space rocks. Most asteroids are made of rock. Asteroids are leftover pieces from when the solar system was formed. Most asteroids in our solar system orbit our Sun.

Sun

asteroid belt

asteroids

Most asteroids live in the asteroid belt. This is an area in our solar system between Mars and Jupiter. The belt is shaped like a doughnut.

There are millions of asteroids floating in the asteroid belt. But all of them put together would still be smaller than our Moon.

asteroids in the asteroid belt

SMART WORD

asteroid: a type of space rock that comes in many shapes and sizes

Asteroid Shapes and Sizes

Asteroids are the odd balls in space. Most asteroids are not round like balls or planets. They are odd-shaped. Some look like lumpy potatoes. Some look like peanuts! Asteroids come in many shapes and sizes.

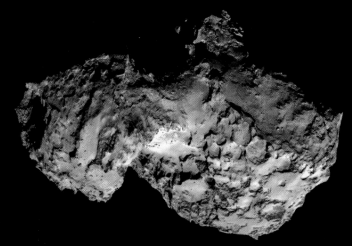

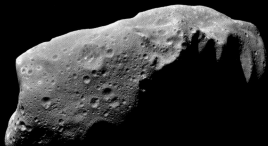

odd-shaped asteroids

different shapes and sizes of asteroids

Vesta, the largest asteroid

Smaller asteroids are odd-shaped. Larger asteroids, like Vesta, are rounder. The bigger an object, the stronger the **gravity** is. Gravity is the force that pulls objects in space together. Most asteroids are too small to have enough gravity to "make themselves" round.

SMART WORD

gravity: the force that pulls objects in space together

A Big Blast!

Kaboom!

Sixty-five million years ago, a huge astero hit Earth. Smoke from fires blocked out the Sun. Plants died, which left nothing for dinosaurs to eat. Scientists think that this asteroid wiped out most life on Earth, including the large dinosaurs.

asteroid crashing into Earth

asteroid hitting Earth

When the asteroid hit Earth, it created a huge **crater**, or hole. The crater was over 100 miles wide!

Chicxulub crater in Mexico's Yucatán

A much smaller asteroid that hit Arizona left a crater almost a mile wide. But the asteroid was only 80 feet long. That's about as long as a basketball court.

SMART WORDS

crater: a large, bowl-shaped hole on a moon or planet usually caused by a crashing space rock

scientist: a person who studies or works in an area of science

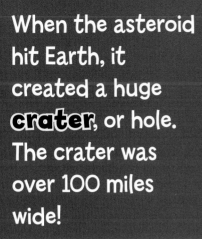
Barringer Crater in Arizona

13

USE YOUR SMART WORDS

Use your Smart Words to complete the crossword.

asteroid   crater   gravity   scientist

Across

2. A person who studies things like asteroids

4. The force that pulls objects in space together

Down

1. A kind of space rock that comes in many shapes and sizes

3. A hole caused by an asteroid or other space rock

WHAT DO YOU KNOW?

How are asteroids and planets the same? How are they different? Copy this Venn diagram. In the left circle, fill in what you learned about asteroids. In the right circle, fill in what you know about planets. In the middle part, fill in the things that they share.

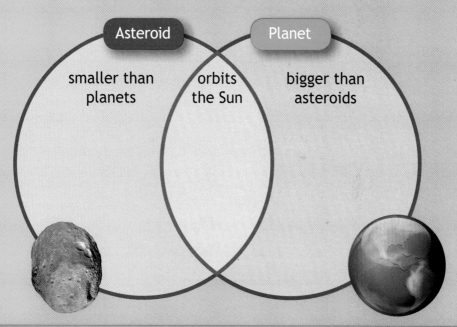

Asteroid

Planet

smaller than planets

orbits the Sun

bigger than asteroids

TALK LIKE A SCIENTIST

Imagine that an asteroid hit Earth. Use your Smart Words to explain what you would do. What would you need to survive?

CHAPTER 3

Icy, Rocky Comets!

Is it a snowball? Is it a ball of fire? No! It's a comet! So what is a **comet**? It's a space rock that looks like a star with hair!

comet

SMART WORD

comet: a space rock made up of ice, dust, and rock that orbits the Sun

A comet is an icy ball of rock and dust orbiting our Sun. In space, it looks like a giant, dirty snowball. It's about the size of a small town!

This is what a comet might look like in space.

When comets are in space far away from the Sun, we cannot see them. That's because they are very far away — way beyond all the planets in our solar system.

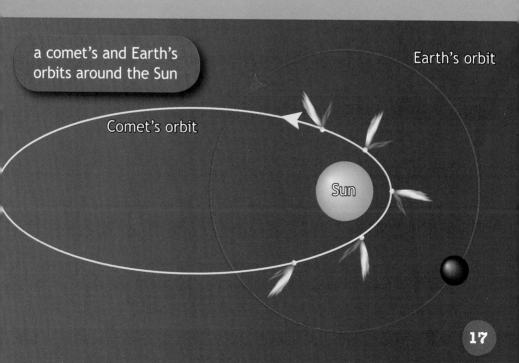

a comet's and Earth's orbits around the Sun

Earth's orbit

Comet's orbit

Sun

Glowing Comets

Without the Sun, we would not see comets. As comets approach the Sun, they start to warm up. The Sun's heat begins to melt the ice. Then something amazing happens. The comets begin to glow very brightly!

Comet Holmes

As comets heat up, they form long bright **tails**. Most comets have two tails. They can be millions of miles long!

parts of a comet

gas tail

head

dust tail

Comets in space can last for thousands of years! Some comets crash into the Sun and disappear. Others fly by and go back into space, only to return again and again.

SMART WORD

tail: the long bright part of a comet

Returning Visitors

The most famous returning visitor is Halley's Comet. It takes 75 years for it to orbit, or travel around, the Sun. We last saw it in 1986. We won't see it again until 2061!

Halley's Comet

Comets may have hit Earth many years ago. Some scientists think that a comet, not an asteroid, hit Earth and caused most dinosaurs to disappear millions of years ago.

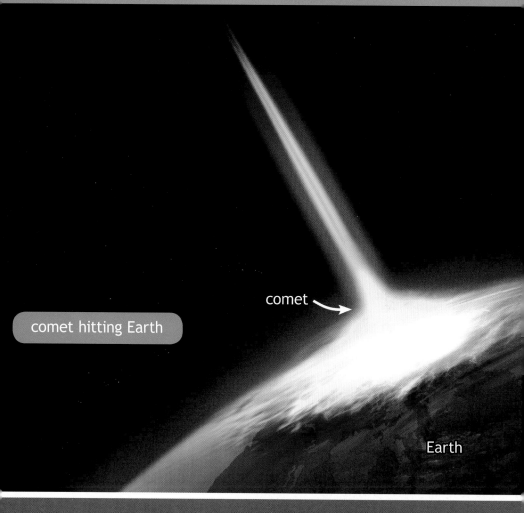

comet

comet hitting Earth

Earth

Scientists have found 4,000 comets in our solar system. That's a lot of space rocks flying around!

USE YOUR

SMART WORDS

On a separate piece of paper, draw a comet. Use your Smart Words to label your drawing. What or who will you name your comet after?

comet   tail

TRUE or FALSE?

Which statements are true? Which are false?

T F

❏ ❏ In space, a comet looks like a dirty snowball.

❏ ❏ A comet has one tail.

❏ ❏ The Sun melts the ice on a comet.

❏ ❏ A comet's tail can never be more than one hundred miles long.

❏ ❏ Halley's Comet is a returning visitor.

❏ ❏ We would not see comets without the Moon.

TALK LIKE A SCIENTIST

You hear on the radio that Halley's Comet will appear in one week. Scientists are preparing a big viewing party. Why would you want to go? Use your Smart Words to explain what a **comet** looks like.

CHAPTER 4

Many, Many Meteors!

A blazing light shoots through the night sky. It is as bright as a star. It moves fast. To some it looks like a shooting star. Could it be a comet? No, it's a meteor. A meteor looks a bit like a comet. But the two space rocks are different.

meteor

A meteor starts out as a **meteoroid**. This is a small piece of rock that breaks off from an asteroid or other space rock. A meteoroid can be as small as a grain of sand or as large as a car.

an asteroid breaking up into meteoroids

Many meteoroids have hit the Moon. That's what caused many of the Moon's craters!

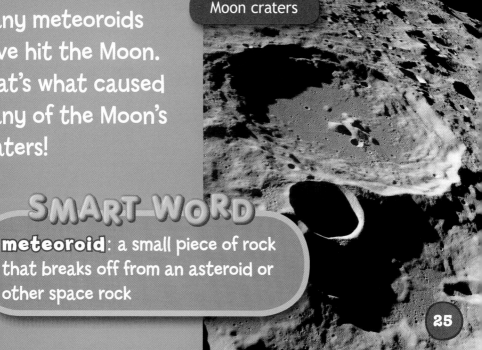
Moon craters

SMART WORD

meteoroid: a small piece of rock that breaks off from an asteroid or other space rock

Meteors

When meteoroids enter Earth's atmosphere, they become **meteors**. Most burn up high in the atmosphere. Some people think they look like shooting stars. But they are not stars at all. When several meteors appear in the same place and time, we get an amazing meteor shower.

SMART-WORD

meteor: a meteoroid that enters Earth's atmosphere

Geminid meteor shower

Sometimes, meteors come very close to crashing into Earth. On February 15, 2013, the Chelyabinsk meteor streaked through the sky in southern Russia. The meteor was almost as long as a bowling lane.

Chelyabinsk meteor streaking through the sky

The meteor exploded before it hit the ground. But the shock wave damaged buildings and injured many people.

What Is a Meteorite?

A **meteorite** is a piece of a meteor that survives and falls to Earth. Many meteorites fall to Earth each day. Most meteorites are tiny — the size of pebbles or dust. That's why we don't even notice them!

meteoroid

space

meteor

atmosphere

meteorite

Earth

A meteoroid is in space. When it enters Earth's atmosphere, it is called a meteor. When it survives and falls to Earth, it is called a meteorite.

But some meteorites can be larger. The 1992 Peekskill meteorite in New York State weighed about as much as a bowling ball. It streaked through the sky as fast as a jet . . . and then crashed into a parked car!

Peekskill meteorite

SMART WORDS

Look at the pictures below. Which one is NOT a space rock?

asteroid

comet

meteoroid

meteor

meteorite

Sun

TALK LIKE A SCIENTIST

Your friend says that he caught a **meteoroid**. Explain why this could or could not happen. Use your Smart Words.

SMART WORDS GLOSSARY

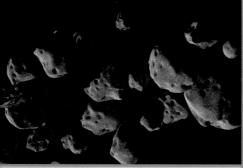

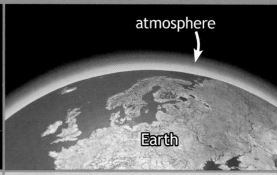

atmosphere

Earth

asteroid: a type of space rock that comes in many shapes and sizes

atmosphere: the layer of air that surrounds a planet

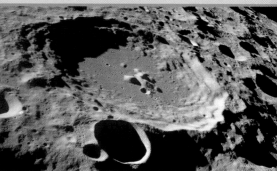

comet: a space rock made up of ice, dust, and rock that orbits the Sun

crater: a hole caused by an asteroid or other space rocks

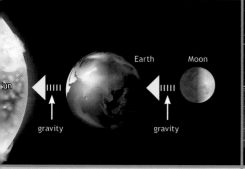

Earth   Moon

un

gravity   gravity

gravity: the force that pulls objects in space together

meteor: a meteoroid that enters Earth's atmosphere

meteorite: a meteor that falls to Earth

meteoroid: a small piece of rock that breaks off from an asteroid or other space rocks

orbit: to travel around something, like the Sun or a planet

scientist: a person who studies or works in an area of science

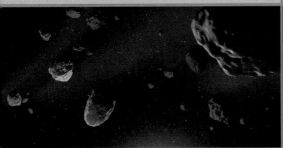

space rock: an object in space made of rock, ice, gas, dust, or metal

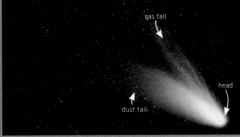

gas tail
head
dust tail

tail: the long bright part of a comet

USE YOUR SMART WORDS ANSWERS

PAGE 6: space rocks, atmosphere, orbit

PAGE 14: ACROSS 2. scientist 4. gravity DOWN 1. asteroid 3. crater

PAGE 23: T, F, T, F, T, F

PAGE 30: Sun